MY PATH OF SILENCE TO RECOVERY

By
Marah R Malgapo

Copyright © 2023 All rights reserved By WMS PRESS

Published in 2023 by Marah Malgapo
Cover Concept: WMS PRESS

All rights reserved. No part of this book may be reproduced, stored, in a retrieval system, or transmitted by any means, electronic, mechanical, photocopying, recording, or otherwise be copied for public or private use (other than for "fair use" as brief quotations embodied in articles and reviews) without prior written permission from the copyright holder.

The author of this book does not prescribe medical advice or promotes the use of any of the techniques as a method for physical, emotional, or medical problems without the advice of a professional, either directly or indirectly. The intent of the author is only to offer information of a general nature to help you in your quest for mental and personal growth. In the event you use any of the information in this book for yourself, the author and the publisher assume no responsibility for your actions.

My Path of Silence to Recovery
Published in 2023 by Marah Malgapo

For any ordering information or
special discounts for bulk purchases,
please contact: marahrmalgapo@gmail.com

Published in 2023 by Marah Malgapo
Copyright © 2023 All rights reserved.

By WMS PRESS
ISBN # 978-1-7356447-6-9

1st edition, May 2023
Printed in Andover, MA

I dedicate this book to my good friend Kira Danielle Parris-Moore. She has been my rock and good friend since childhood. She stuck by me through thick and thin. She even saved my life a few times. She was able to have me be free of my silence after over a year of one of my traumas. She is such a strong, loving, loyal friend, and I am so lucky I have met her. I moved my big violin on the bus, so she had somewhere to sit, because she was the last stop. I am so glad I did that. She is also an author for children and mental health https://books2inspire.com Please check it out. Children may not know what is out there and it will help you as a guardian to relate and discuss mental health issues while your child is still young.

CONTENTS

Prologue vii

Chapter 1: Being Adopted. 1

Chapter 2: Family. 3

Chapter 3: Friends in Elementary School 5

Chapter 4: Middle School. 7

Chapter 5: My First True Love. 9

Chapter 6: First Attack .11

Chapter 7: Second Attack. 15

Chapter 8: Third Attack 19

Chapter 9: Fourth Attack 23

Chapter 10: One of My Ex Best Friends 27

Chapter 11: My Mental Health 29

Chapter 12: The Hospital 33

Chapter 13: Rehab 35

Chapter 14: My Fistula. 37

Chapter 15: Theft. 41

Chapter 16: Apartments 43

Chapter 17: Seeking Help 45

Chapter 18: My Ex-Husband 47

Chapter 19: The Boyfriend 51

Chapter 20: Being Free 55

Chapter 21: My Parents 57

Chapter 22: Survivor 59

Chapter 23: End of the Year 61

Chapter 24: The New Year 71

   About the Author 73

   Resources 74

PROLOGUE

I AM WRITING this book for survivors. For people who are silent and are scared to come out. For all those non-reported incidences. And this is to show it can take less than 27 years to have a voice. How people make you feel shameful, scared, and not know where or who to go to. How the justice system is not strong and makes the victim feel powerless. You are not alone. There are many people out there who need to share their story and need a safe place to go and need support emotionally, physically, and legally.

CHAPTER 1

BEING ADOPTED

HI, I AM a 43-year-old who was adopted at 16 months old. I was adopted through Love the Children. My mother had a friend at school where she taught who had already adopted a Korean baby and recommended it. My mother said she wanted a baby girl, so she made an inquiry to the company. The first day of Hanukkah in 1980, my mother received information and a picture of me. My parents were ecstatic.

While I was in Korea, I was told that my birth mother was very poor and unable to take care of me, so I had a foster mother. I found out not long after that my birth father was an alcoholic. Then, in April 1981, I flew into JFK airport in New York. They said, "List baby." My mother, father, aunt, and uncle waited for me. My aunt gave me a pink elephant, which I still have today.

Coming home there was a big welcome home party. Lots of family and friends came to celebrate. I have been told I was very hungry and ate three eggs! I was 16 months at that time. My mother said every time I went into the crib I started crying, so she held me all through the night. This is when abandonment issues were being managed in my new home. I needed that connection.

CHAPTER 2

FAMILY

I WAS VERY close to my parents and brother, who was 10 years older and my parents' natural son. We played together, but once he hit high school he changed. He was on varsity lacrosse and hockey, had several parties and lots of friends. On the way back from family gatherings he offered me money to be quiet, mostly because I liked to talk and ask a lot of questions. We went to lots of family events and vacations. Everything was great.

Then he went to college. I remember I was only eight years old. I was home alone in the kitchen when he was leaving. He had big bags with him he was carrying to the car. I was so sad. When he left, I cried. I wished he was around. Maybe if he was, I would have told him what happened to me. I'll never know.

CHAPTER 3

FRIENDS IN ELEMENTARY SCHOOL

I FELT LIKE I had so many friends up till middle school. My mom was a teacher, and everyone knew her. I had five best friends, did Hebrew school three times a week, dance twice a week, and violin one day a week. I had a learning disability, however, and speech problems. It also didn't help that at the age of four, I had seizures. I didn't get off medicine until I was 12. So, I was lucky I did most of my homework in my special ed class.

There was one girl, however, who became my special friend in elementary school. She was the last bus stop and there were no more seats. So, I moved my violin and let her sit next to me. She became my advocate, my friend, my voice. I was quiet and shy around people who weren't a part of my circle, still a little true to this day. The first time I remember meeting her was when I was giving out my

Bubblicious gum to people and ended up with none for myself; she stood up for me.

And later years she saved me and gave me the courage to do things that a teenager should never face alone. She helped me get up at my 40th birthday when I was incapacitated on the floor and again when I was 42 and almost dead. I was told I was lying in vomit barely breathing. She's the main reason I am still around today to tell my story.

My father lost his job and started working temp jobs. We didn't go to so many family gatherings, vacations, and dance classes. The transition from elementary school to middle school was the worst. My so-called five best friends stopped talking to me. I wasn't cool enough to go to a Duran Duran concert or watch 90210. And my stalker and traumas began. When I got *The Little Mermaid*, I watched it every day after school for a year. These were my last happy moments as a child before it all started.

CHAPTER 4

MIDDLE SCHOOL

IN 6TH GRADE, I had barely any friends. Instead, I hung out and had lunch with an 8th grader. Once she left, I used to eat lunch with my English teacher.

This is when it all started. Every day in 6th and 7th grade when I left orchestra class and made that left turn to my next class, this boy came with a few of his friends and used to jump on my back. I already had a huge double zipper LL Bean backpack. He startled me, but I didn't think it was necessary to tell a teacher. I mean, what am I going to say, someone is jumping on my back?

When I was 13, I moved to the third floor and got my own phone line. It was a dial-up number for the internet as well. I had a birthday slumber party and they dared me to hump a lamp. I had no idea what hump meant. They tried to explain it, so I did. My pelvic bone hurt afterward. Through these new friends I met with a few boys on the phone. One was mean and scary. The other two were nice. Twenty-nine years later I am still talking to them. We used to be on three-way-calling for eight hours a day. One of them I fell for hard; my first true love.

One hot day, in the summer of 1994, he rode his bike to my house. When I saw him, I knew he was the one.

CHAPTER 5

MY FIRST TRUE LOVE

IT MUST HAVE been spring 1994 when we started talking. I favored him for some reason. So, that Summer 1994 we met and I fell in love. We were also on the phone for hours. That November he came over and I knew it was going to happen. We were sitting in the closet in the dark. He asked me to kiss him, so I kissed him like in the movies. I totally messed up. Didn't know what I was doing.

So, after that it took years for me to have the confidence to kiss again. It became sweet soft pecks after that, years later. I never made out like in the movies again. We saw each other on and off for 29 years. He was so gentle, smooth, and considerate, always asking if I was okay. I trusted him and would do anything he asked me to do.

This past summer, June 2022, I asked him a question about his friend who came by on

2/21/95, and he denied knowing anything about it.

During the winter storm of 1996, when school was closed, I took two buses to go see him. Nothing would ever stop me from talking to or seeing this man. When he moved to his senior year, I found him. We met up. Then he did something that scared me, so I left. Then, many years later, I found him on Facebook and messaged him. Then we had an affair. I always end up going back to him. No matter where we live, regardless of our status, jobs, no matter what, we always end up talking again.

CHAPTER 6

FIRST ATTACK

FEBRUARY 21, 1995, my first true love came over with his friend who was 19. I had just turned 15. My first love told me to go upstairs and he would be there in a bit. So, I went up to my room with his friend. This guy made me do things I didn't want to do. He put his penis in my mouth and I couldn't breathe; it barely fit in my mouth, and it smelled like fish. I tried to pull away, but he forced my head on it deeper and I gagged. He kept my head down. I don't even remember how, but he attacked me. I still remember his heavy body on me. I was maybe 90 lbs. at that time. I remember his heavy breathing, moaning, his hot breath on my face. He was so rough, going deep and hard and fast, invading parts of me that had never been touched. I told him he was hurting me and to stop. But he kept going. He went faster and harder every time I told him to stop. I literally felt like I would rather die than be in that situation. I felt like a slut; dirty, ashamed, alone, and scared.

When it was over, I asked where my first love was, and he said he was getting orange juice. I was thinking, *It doesn't take that long to get some orange juice.* I felt like I had cheated on my first love and felt dirty and like a skank. I kept it a secret. I felt so ashamed.

MY VIOLIN

I play the violin
The notes are my words
The volume and pitch are my intensity
My bow is the stimuli
My rosin is the bond of respect
My fingers are my sentences
I speak through music

CHAPTER 7

SECOND ATTACK

THE BOY WHO used to jump on my back was reintroduced to me that same day 2/21/95 in the park that afternoon. My friend was there and she said they were rivals in Virginia Beach and he was upset that I got with my first love. The guy said he jumped on my back because he liked me. So, I thought that was okay.

That August I was at his apartment, although I don't remember how I got there. He was giving me a tour of the apartment and we ended up in the basement with multiple gas meters on the far wall. He cornered me in the left far corner. I don't even remember what he was saying. I know he had his hands around my neck tight and was choking me, demanding that I did as I was told. And he attacked me. Again, I felt dirty and really didn't want to tell anyone. This was the second attack in 1995 when I was 15 years old. I felt so alone, sad, scared, embarrassed, and violated. I thought I would die if I didn't do what he told me.

When he was done, I tried to run away. I was in panic mode, scared as hell. I finally found the exit after being lost in the building for some time. I ran across the main street to my house. I even passed by the street my middle school history teacher lived in. I almost went in, but what was I going to say? The boy said not to tell anyone. My dad thought I was buying school supplies with my friend. I didn't want to get into trouble.

In my special ed class in high school, people were making fun of me and kept going at it. I flipped out and the teacher told my parents. My mom asked if I got assaulted. By this point, I had three guys who'd had a piece of me. I played like I only had sex once. I didn't want anyone to know the other stuff. I didn't know how to tell them. I felt like a slut. So, I told her no, he did not assault me.

One of my best friends and I went to see *Waiting to Exhale*. At the end of the movie, she asked me if that individual assaulted me. I was wondering how she knew. She told me he tried to do the same to her. I felt so close to her for knowing what happened without me saying the words. Even to this day, I can't say it.

Sometime in 1996, a year after the fact, I told the police and they basically laughed at me and said there was no evidence. This is a sonnet I wrote my sophomore year about this individual.

SECRET PRISON

He treated her as if she were a slave
She felt like she was a lost puppy dog
She was too weak to even become brave
She was confused in a storm with much fog
She felt like she was a trapped animal
She was locked in her house without a key
All of the hurt just became way too full
She was too ashamed to let people see
She wanted help but where would she get it?
She was suffering from paranoia
With people and herself it was a fit
She felt like a sheep that cannot say, "Baa"
This has been a secret for much too long
Even to this day, it's just a sad song

CHAPTER 8

THIRD ATTACK

I WAS DATING this guy. He was nice. We were celebrating Christmas December 1999. He got me cucumber melon body wash and lotion from Bath and Body Works. Then I remember being in his bedroom. The plan was to get intimate for the first time, so we did, and I wanted it to stop; he was hurting me. He was 300 lbs. and six feet tall. I was 90 lbs. and five feet tall. I told him to stop because he was hurting me. All I remember is his heavy body on me, breathing heavily, his hot breath on my face; he said he was almost done, just a little bit longer. I scratched him and somehow used my legs to kick him.

I had learned from my previous experiences and I went directly to the police. We had a court date, but he didn't show up. The judge asked if he raped me. I couldn't answer. I said, "I think so."

She said, "Did he or did he not?" in a scary voice.

I said, "I don't know." I mean come on; you're telling me it's really rape when it happened three times?

So, my attacker was a no show, but I got a restraining order. I felt safe with that. I just didn't want to see him or have him near me. I felt strong and powerful.

ONE LAST RAPE

Rape my heart to pieces
Torture the innocence of wanting to be loved
And to love
No one asked you to take advantage of me

Rape my soul
Torture the other half to make me whole
And to complete you
No one permitted you to misuse it

Rape my mind
Torture the sane thinking of me
And to help you through the time of rationality
No one requested you to trespass and control me

CHAPTER 9

FOURTH ATTACK

I WAS PLANNING on seeing my first love again. I was married at that point and having an affair. He denied me; I got mad. At this point of my life, he never denied me. So, I called up this guy that I had known since I was 16. He hadn't done anything bad to me since. He co-owned a restaurant. I believe it was Route 31 in Sparta IL, the mid island on the left.

We met, had lunch, and I had four martinis. He asked if I wanted to see his house and to rest. I said yes. I told my husband that I was with a friend and we were watching a movie. We were watching *The Waterboy* for a few minutes, and he had several young guys in his house. I assumed that he was renting it out to them. Then we were in his bedroom. I'm not sure what happened. I just know he was on top of me, and I was very sore after. My stomach was in so much pain. I don't know if I said anything. I just wanted to rest.

I know later, when he brought me back to the restaurant where my car was, I went to urgent care, but they wouldn't do a pelvic exam. They told me to go to the ER or my OB. So, I went to another urgent care, and he wouldn't do a pelvic exam either. I just said I had severe abdominal pain and he prescribed ibuprofen 600 mg. I then went to my OB and she did an exam a few days later and said everything looked okay.

One time, weeks later, my husband and I were out having pizza and I told him what happened. He wanted to press charges, but I didn't want to. I didn't remember if I had said no or told him to stop. My husband was jealous. He thought we hooked up in college, but we didn't. He found out he helped me move my stuff out of my dorm and jumped to conclusions.

STEAL FROM ME

Steal from me

Hear my voice scream

Steal from me

Hear the past creep up

Steal from me

Hear the cries of unjust

Steal from me

Throw salt on my wounds

Steal from me

CHAPTER 10

ONE OF MY EX BEST FRIENDS

I HAD A best friend, and we did everything together. We went to water parks, cruises, beaches, and lunch. She was a teacher and I worked three days a week, so in the summer we were always together.

She posted a photo on Facebook asking people to vote for her and her husband as the best married couple of the year. My other best friend said they weren't and then the two of them started fighting. Then, one day, my ex best friend called me several times. But I had to get up at 5:00 a.m. and if I got on the phone with her, I would be on the phone for at least two hours. It was already 10:30 p.m., past my bedtime. She accused me of saying something I didn't, something along the lines of making fun of her friend who had food stamps. I would never make fun of someone on those lines. So, after years passed in which I sent letters and emails and took stuff to her house and left it at the front door, I accepted that she wasn't as good of a friend as I had thought. She should have known me better than to make that kind of comment.

I tried multiple times to contact and reconnect. Nothing. So I went into a great depression. I wanted to commit suicide. I phoned my psychiatrist and told him, but he said he was on his way to a vacation when I called. I ended up being involuntarily committed to a psych unit. Another major abandonment.

CHAPTER 11

MY MENTAL HEALTH

I WAS IN the psych unit for almost a month. I had to get a lawyer to get me out and we are still friends today. My symptoms back then, however, included insomnia, great depression, excessive spending, wanting to be intimate with my first love all the time, and suicidal thoughts. Later, with my first love, I became manic. Losing this friend was such heartache, worse than breaking up with a boyfriend. I thought I had her forever. I was the matron of honor at her wedding and couldn't even see her wedding photos. Now she is married to a guy I introduced her to and she has a little girl.

I ended up being hospitalized in a mental institute five times in 10 years for attempted suicide. I abused alcohol and pills. It was always a one-day attempt, but none of the hospitals and IOP helped me. The only thing that helped was mindful meditation. They diagnosed me as bipolar. The end of March of 2022, when I was packing, I found the restraining order from 1999, which made me extremely depressed. I was upset after so many years, still stuck in this cycle of violence. My plan was to drink and take my Klonopin. But this time I wasn't married and I didn't have someone see me and take me to the hospital.

On March 22, 2022, I called my job, saying I was going to be out for a long time. I have two split-second memories of that week. First, I went to Jersey City to meet my boyfriend and he didn't answer my calls or texts. I knocked on his door and his mom told me he'd said he would be right back. After waiting for over an hour I texted him, saying he must have better things to do that were more important. This was now the second time he refused to communicate and not meet up with me. He promised he wouldn't do that again, but ultimately I ended things. Secondly, I remember talking to my therapist, curled up in a fetal position on the floor.

The things I do not remember that week prior to being admitted to the hospital are getting involved in a car accident, going to the ER three times that week, spending over $1000 at Verizon Wireless on two separate occasions, and a hotel transaction. Also, somehow I ended up in New York, drunk and crying, with a plan to jump off a bridge. I called my first love at 3:00 a.m.; he calmed me down and met me at my apartment at 5:00 a.m. and stayed with me till he had to go to work. He has always secretly been my safety net.

I told him I have unconditional love for him. That he saved my life and was my safety net all those years. I will always have love for him. I know he and I won't work as a couple though. Probably because I never told him how I felt. I can't make anything out of this.

So, I believe my ex-boyfriend assisted in my drinking and/or pills and stole from me. As I said before, I would excessively drink or do an overdose of pills in one day and end up in the ER. This went on for several days. I know someone, probably him, stole my TV and air conditioners and other stuff. That's all I could see when the movers moved my stuff into the storage unit. I believe the Verizon Wireless $1000 was him too. He was always tight with money. I bought him a refrigerator last year and canceled three times. My friends said not to do it.

He found me on a dating site and desperately wanted to see me. He was asking what happened and if I remembered anything. I said no. The next week, he came to see me. Then he wanted to come again. I told him I had a boyfriend and he couldn't come visiting like that anymore. Once I found his name on 3/22/22 on my calendar and I asked him if he came to see me. He cut me off and said I had mental issues, to never contact him again, and he blocked me. I went to the police and made a report that week and they said there was no proof. They said just because he blocked me it didn't mean anything happened.

When I first went to rehab on 5/20/22, I got a phone call from the cops telling me to come by. I went in and they said two reports had been made about me. The first was from 3/25/22 when I was at Verizon Wireless. Someone had called the police because I was crying, bruised up, and confused. The second was from 3/29/22. One of my best friends had called me and I hadn't answered and I always answered her calls. She told my mom, who told my brother, who lives in Maryland. He tried calling but got no answer. He called 911 for a safety check. The police report showed that I was sitting on my bed gazing and unresponsive and there was no signs of alcohol or pills. When my brother went to my apartment, he said there were pills and alcohol everywhere. My ex-husband said I was lying on the floor in a pool of vomit.

CHAPTER 12

THE HOSPITAL

I WAS ADMITTED to the hospital on 3/29/22. I was in a coma for about a week. I was on a ventilator and had no brain activity. I am told they were going to pull the plug. My uncle told me he was preparing to come to my funeral. I had visitors and people praying for me. They said the next day I had brain activity. It was a miracle. I remember opening my eyes on 4/5/22. I remember seeing my mom, aunt, and uncle. My brother, sister-in-law, ex-husband, his girlfriend and mother, and some close friends visited. Others came when I was in a coma and prayed for me. It truly was a miracle.

In the two months of being in the hospital I had kidney disease, was on dialysis, had blood pressure in the 180s, a resting heart rate in the 150s, failed my swallow test for a month, lost 20 lbs., had pneumonia and a GI bleed, had to receive blood, and developed foot drop. My feet were in so much pain. Because I had overdosed, the doctors wouldn't give me opioids, and because of my kidneys I was limited as to what I could take. So, all I had was Tylenol. I told every individual about my foot pain, and it wasn't managed till months later. I told every individual that came into my room how bad my pain was. The neurologist said he would order something but he only did at the very end. I got three one-time Percocet orders that only took the edge off. I was still in a lot of pain.

The week before they medically cleared me, I had physical therapy. I couldn't turn on my own or move. My legs and feet couldn't move. The aides were so good and did a passive range of motion and massaged my feet. With physical therapy I was shaking when standing up and only able to take two steps.

On 5/20/22 they discharged me medically and mentally. Due to my mental illness, I got denied access to multiple rehabs. They put me on their voluntary psych unit until they could find me a place to move to that was more suitable for my needs. My brother felt like I needed 24-hour care, so I was able to get into the rehab associated with the hospital after an appeal.

CHAPTER 13

REHAB

NURSES, AIDES, THERAPISTS, doctors, nurses, practitioners, and housekeeping, everyone was coming into my room. There was absolutely no privacy or peace in which to nap; I only slept four hours a night. About four months in I finally got my braces and was able to walk much better. Still, it was only 100 feet or so before I would get tired. The physical therapist showed me how to use my feet to assist with getting around in the wheelchair.

During that time, I met someone on a dating site. He said he loved me for me. I still had two missing teeth and a wheelchair, and he still took good care of me. Such a gentleman. Today, we are celebrating our three-month anniversary. He spends so much money and I feel bad. We see each other twice a week because I told him once a week isn't enough.

In June 2022, my short-term disability ended. I was denied long-term disability, but I got approved for Social Security in late

October 2022. I'm just waiting for the letter of approval.

My parents moved me to an assisted living facility shortly after to help me open up to my traumas. I wish I could talk to my mom about them, but I don't want to stress them out and they probably don't remember how things were back then. My brother and I were having problems; he seemed to only contact me when he had a reason, a purpose, like a business transaction. Even though he wasn't very nice in the email he sent me, I sent two nice emails; I let my guard down and explained to him how everything was making me feel. Because of all of this he volunteered to help and became my power of attorney and health proxy. I will forever be grateful. And all my assets will go to him when I pass.

Things are good now. He sold my car, deposited the check into my checking account, and gave me my keys, wallet, safe and laptop. Things are much better. I don't contact him unless there is something medical happening or I really need help and advice. I don't go to my family for help. I go to my extended family—my friends.

CHAPTER 14

MY FISTULA

THREE WEEKS AGO, my nephrologist talked to me about getting a fistula. She originally believed this was reversible. Further blood work says something different. That Wednesday, I was supposed to go to the ER to wait for surgery. I had my COVID booster the day before and I was feverish, with a heart rate of 130. I was able to take Tylenol and the medicine that slows down my heart rate and felt better.

That Friday, at dialysis, I asked about the surgery. They promised me before 9:00 p.m. I hadn't eaten since 5:00 a.m. When being transferred to the ER I was tearing up. I felt like I had no choice; I had to do it or I would die. It reminded me of 2/21/95. Having a choice but forced against it. And feeling like I would rather die than be in the situation. I felt like those were the only options.

At 8:40 p.m. they rolled me down to the OR waiting area. Nurses were complaining that they wanted to go home. The doctor said he had done 10 surgeries in 12 hours and he had four more cases after me.

The surgeon was able to identify the veins he was going to use by looking at my arm. I had never heard of or seen a fistula so low in the arm. It was going to be on my right forearm, wrist, and hand. I was going to have the surgery.

In the operating room, he painted my arm and hand with Betadine and within seconds I fell asleep, had the surgery and was moved to post op. Later on, that fistula stopped working. I should have listened to my gut.

I got onto the floor. My neighbor had such a loud ring on her phone and it kept ringing. There were people talking in the speakers and hallways, and the light in the hallways was bright. I couldn't sleep. I was supposed to leave that Saturday between 2:00 and 5:00 p.m. That was what the social worker said. The transportation kept pushing it to 7:00 p.m., 8:00 p.m., and then sometime later that night. But they never came. The nurse did something with my new roommate at 4:00 a.m. but was quiet and respectful. I called the ambulance at this time, and they said they would be there at 8:00 a.m. Nothing. So, the nurse got transportation via wheelchair. I got back early Sunday afternoon.

Once I came back to my room, the nurse said he needed to take the blood pressure in my leg because the hospital said my fistula was in my left arm. I showed him it was in my right. He kept going by what he was told. He couldn't make his own assessment.

Every day I told the nurse my fistula was hot, painful, and swollen. They said it looked good, so they did nothing. Because of that, I developed a blister. At exactly two weeks post op I saw my nephrologist in dialysis and showed her. I explained what had happened. She couldn't believe it; she gave me her personal cell number. Within 10 minutes I got blood cultures done as a stat dose of Ancef. Vancomycin IV the next day and labs on Monday pre-dialysis. I texted her a pic of my fistula. Then she ordered vancomycin with every dialysis for the next week.

CHAPTER 15

THEFT

WITHIN MAYBE A two-to-three week bracket I had four things stolen from me. First, my former mother-in-law wrote me a beautiful letter and gave me a crucifix. The letter said to put it under my pillow, so I did. Within a week it went missing. For my one-month anniversary with my boyfriend I bought us two matching tiger eye bracelets. That, too, went missing. Last Saturday, I had my Valentino perfume in my purse. I was getting ready on Tuesday to see my boyfriend and I noticed it was missing. Last, my friend's birthday gift. Someone took it out of the Amazon box and left the box in my room according to housekeeping, who said she threw out an empty box.

CHAPTER 16

APARTMENTS

I HAVE BEEN looking at several apartments in low-income areas. I found two in New Brunswick and one in Monroe. There was a 55+ in Highland Park. If they get back to me, I'll tell them I'm in a wheelchair with no family or husband. We'll see. I have more support in Middlesex County.

CHAPTER 17

SEEKING HELP

SINCE JUNE I have been trying to find a trauma therapist who will take my insurance. I asked my psychiatrist and nurse practitioner. My current therapist is encouraging me to get a trauma therapist. In some areas I think I need more help. I even spoke to the prosecutor's office, special victim unit, and rape advocates, but they denied me as well. So, I started writing therapy, which is helping. I don't want my boyfriend to see me so tired and not feeling good because I am in a rehab facility and no one can help me. My friend told me about this one lady who does writing therapy, unlicensed, and at a reasonable price. So, for now that is what I am doing.

CHAPTER 18

MY EX-HUSBAND

I DATED MY ex-husband on and off since 1997. He really wasn't my type. It took two years for the first kiss, and even at that he lied to me. He promised me he wouldn't kiss me on my lips. He was always doing car things, hanging out at Dunkin' Donuts until 3:00 a.m., and going to car shows. When I was studying, his mom told me to stay over if it was getting late; I was always at his house. His mom would cook for us, and I started to go to family gatherings. The next step was to get married, but his mom and cars always came first.

On my wedding day, he promised he would see me before I walked down the aisle. On the day in question, he didn't. He said one of my friends advised him not to, it's bad luck. I told him I didn't care. He had made a promise to me. I was so upset. I cried six times on my wedding day. I almost didn't walk down that aisle. The manager and my dad were trying to calm me down. Once I saw him, I relaxed.

During the wedding reception, I was mostly with my friends, and he was with his.

He was like ¾ my best friend, but I still didn't tell him everything. As a person, a friend, he was good aside from his jealousy. His jealousy, controlling behavior, and having his mom and cars a priority over me destroyed us. In time, I found my first true love on Facebook; we started messaging and met up. We started to have an affair. My first love was my true love, my safety net for decades. My ex-husband found out when I was texting beside him in bed, he took a screenshot around my shoulder.

In marriage counseling I didn't deny it. That's one thing, I do not lie. He still wanted things to work out. But my heart was with my first love. I didn't want anything to do with this marriage and all the problems we had. Later, I believed I was manic. In the end, I would see my first love three times a week. I was obsessing over him.

Over the past 10 years, my ex-husband was with me each of the four times I tried to commit suicide. He was so good to me. He would visit at every visiting hour. Even in a terrible snowstorm he visited me at one of the hospitals I was at. I could always depend on him, but I wasn't in love with him. One time, when I was at an IOP, I was on a high dose of Latuda. He believed that was the drug that made me love him. Once I was discharged, my outpatient psychiatrist said it prevented me from sleeping and took me off it. My ex-husband begged the psychiatrist to put me back on it.

I found out on October 17, 2022 that he had remarried. They got pregnant within three months of dating. She is controlling and manipulative. She doesn't want me talking to him anymore. He told me he was going to be busy moving his company to another location.

In the past four months he hasn't responded to my messages on Instagram or email since he blocked me. His doctor called me, saying he needs to reschedule. The office left a message, calling me by his wife's name. I called them back and said, "This is not her, this is his ex-wife." The office apologized and said my ex-husband was not answering his phone and to email him and that he was going to take me and my number off as his emergency contact.

When their baby was born, they created an Instagram and I blocked it. I don't want to know about or see anything they're doing now. I know with a baby, her Filipino culture, and her being so controlling I'll never see or talk to him again.

His mother is the one who got me into nursing. I studied, ate, and slept. Whenever I passed a test, I went with my good friend to the Cheesecake Factory and got a pear martini. This is really where the drinking began, since I never really drank before then. At the time, wine was too tart, so I took a liking to martinis instead.

CHAPTER 19

THE BOYFRIEND

SO, I WAS on a dating app and found this man. He and I had a similar upbringing. Both adopted, both had trauma. He was 50 years old and seemed intimidating at 6'3". And he was half Italian and half British. I was very honest from the beginning and told him I don't like Italian men. And he agreed, naming similar attributes. So, we took it slow.

After a few dates I asked him how he felt about becoming exclusive and he had similar feelings. We made it official 7/26/22. He was so sweet and thoughtful, brought me food, flowers, and smiles. But after a month we had a problem. It was his birthday. His best female friend bought him body wash, body lotion, cologne, and deodorant. She, 29 at the time, said he likes to smell nice. She was in an unhappy two-year relationship with her guy. My boyfriend at the time said she and other girls he used to hang out with at the club would sleep with someone. He told me he usually waited until the third date. One time, they were planning on going out to the club. He told me they were leaving at 9:00 p.m. and would be home by midnight. I texted around 11:00 and he said they were leaving. What were they doing for two hours? I didn't sleep that night. He texted me at 3:00 a.m. saying he was just getting in because his friend has ADHD and changes her mind so many times.

So, he told me he would update me when he hung out with her. I never told him he couldn't hang out with her or go to the club. That was his lifestyle before. Those were his choices. He also told me he took an Uber from East Brunswick to her place in Jersey City, to the club in Newark, took her home and then went to his home. I asked him why she couldn't take her own Uber. He said it was dangerous. This woman could have been his daughter given the age difference. Once in a relationship you would think he would want to change just to avoid conflict. He didn't like a guy I talked to, so I stopped. Just out of respect for his feelings.

So, two months went by, and things were going well, except for the same problem. He went to the club for a Halloween party and got home at around 1:00 a.m. That was okay. Then we had our second argument. I was talking and he interrupted, raising his voice saying he was talking now. So, I let him say what he had to say. Basically, he said he couldn't afford to see me twice a week, which would be difficult. He said he had spent $1800 on Ubers in one month on transportation. I said he could lease or finance a car for less. He said with insurance it was about the same cost.

In the end he just didn't want to come twice a week. So, I listened to what he had to say and hung up. We didn't talk until the next day. He texted me good morning. I waited 15 minutes, debating whether or not I should reply and eventually I did. I went out with my friend Kenny for his birthday dinner. In the meantime, my boyfriend was making plans with his best female friend to go to a seafood restaurant in Kenilworth, which is only two towns over, behind my back. He could have picked me up. He promised me he would update me with plans with this best female friend. I wanted to talk and work things out. But he made plans with her and her dad. I didn't want his money. He texted me saying he would make it work and would come see me and said something about 8:20. He didn't show up, so I texted him around 8:45 and said, "I guess you're not coming." He waited a half hour and said he was with her at the restaurant. So, now he had yelled at me and lied. I sent him a screenshot of his message saying he would see me.

I texted him and said, "Well, you made your choice. What's your address or your work address so I can send you your Christmas gift? If you don't reply, I'll throw it in the garbage." I posted on my Facebook page the "Loungin" video by LL Cool J and Total and posted that after two strikes you're out. Two days later, there was still no response. He blocked me. So, I printed out a return label for his Christmas gift. It was going to be returned later that day. I then created a list of nine reasons not to go back with him. And the fact that he yelled at me and lied; I will never take him back. My dad never raised his voice at me. He treated me like a princess. So, this is my requirement for me and my self-worth. And some man must match this, or I'd rather be single.

CHAPTER 20

BEING FREE

MONDAY AND TUESDAY I was unable to sleep. I did my meditation three times in a row. Nothing. But the next few days, I slept so well. Then I went out on Thursday. I had a fun time. I started a dating app again. Within one hour, I had seven messages. I tried to contact two other individuals I knew, but no response. In the meantime, I had my friend I saw on Thursday to help me. After a day I canceled my dating app. I don't know if I want to worry about trust and responsibilities now. I may just hang low and have my friend that I talk to and hang out with occasionally.

I used to obsess over past friendships and loves. But I have accepted that my first love, ex-husband, and ex-boyfriend are doing what they want to do. I wish them nothing but happiness. And I'm doing the same. Just don't know what route to take. But I'll be okay....

CHAPTER 21

MY PARENTS

MY MOM IS 81 and my father 86. My mom is forgetful and anxious. My dad has dementia. I still love them so much. I miss my parents. They aren't the same. I don't want to stress them out with my problems; however, I wish they were around and I could tell them my story. They're too fragile. I don't want them to worry. I wish I could tell my whole story to someone. I don't have anyone I can tell. Maybe that's why I am writing this book.

CHAPTER 22

SURVIVOR

I HAVE ENCOUNTERED loss, abandonment issues, traumas, attacks and, being in the cycle of violence. No one knows my whole story. This book aims to help other individuals that may be facing similar issues. You are not alone. Reporting attacks is scary, but it can lead to justice in your favor. Please tell someone, a friend, family member, therapist, or the police. It's a lot to handle for one person to keep it all inside. I think I finally got out of this cycle of violence. I have kept my whole story a secret for 27 years, but it's too much to carry on alone. Please tell someone.

To help me cope, one of my best friends suggested that I write a letter to my ex, getting my feelings down on paper. So I tried.

CHAPTER 23

END OF THE YEAR

11/26/22
Dear Shawn,

I WANTED TO talk to you, but after so many years I don't have the courage. So, one of my best friends said to write you a letter. You were and are my first everything. Even after all our differences, moving to different locations and changes of status, I always had you in my heart and found you. Even during that terrible winter storm in 1996 I came to see you. I remember in June when we had that argument you said I chose Bobby. Was that a sign you wanted me to choose you? In the many years we have known each other, I thought all you wanted was to do was hook up. But in my heart, it was always more. I loved and still love you so much. I love you unconditionally either way.

You've always been the one since you rode your bike to my house. I knew then that you were going to be the one. I didn't want to scare you away with this letter. Like I said to you, I forgot what it was like to be with a man; you agreed to be that person as I trust you and can be vulnerable. Every time we're together it reminds me of the first time and erases all of my trauma. And then later, when I asked if you wanted to see me, you said all I wanted was to hook up; that is not true. You have secretly been my safety net for 27 years. I always needed you to be there, and you made me feel safe. Whenever I think of my trauma or get triggered, I need you around. I feel like you care for my well-being. But romantically I don't know where you stand.

I just wish I knew what you want from me. I can be your friend, girlfriend, or lover. Whatever you want from me, just tell me. I mean you get upset when I talk about other guys, saying it's not your business. A friend wouldn't mind these conversations; I tell our mutual friend and several of my other friends know what's going on. But I think it bothers you.

So, come out of your shell and tell me what you want from me. I did. I'm risking being rejected. I'll know where I stand. You were and will always be my first love and safety net. So, remember I love you unconditionally, so whatever your answer is and whatever you want from me I can accept and respect it.

Love always,
Marilyn

Two weeks later, Shawn didn't respond to my letter. I knew he wouldn't. He would never directly hurt my feelings. I got sick, positive blood cultures in dialysis. The doctor thought I had endocarditis, the permacath being the source of my infection. I texted him, saying I was in the hospital. He sent prayers my way. Later in the week, he asked how I was doing. He called me "missy." I felt like we might be communicating better. I told him my last memory of him was when I gave him shower-proof Bluetooth speakers but he left them along with his cigarettes on my table. He said he came back and got them, which I don't remember. I'm upset that I don't remember our last encounter.

I also texted my ex-boyfriend to tell him that I was in the hospital. He was sad, or at least his emojis were. Later, he responded that he was trying to find a kidney donor for his sister or she would die. He said I didn't trust him, and he hated this relationship, so I didn't respond.

I was being nosey and looking around Facebook one day. I looked under Shawn's page, which I am sure he prevents people who aren't his friend from seeing. But his "cousin" who he had introduced to me on 2/21/95 was there. He has a crazy long name but the shortened version, how he was introduced to me, was the same. I used a site to find out more information about him. He lived in the same town as I was told he lived in when I met him, was about the same age as me, and had one criminal offense, which was not listed. He was not on the New Jersey Sex Offender website.

When I saw his picture on Facebook, he looked so kind and nice. But I know what he did to me. He was my first attacker; he hurt me, violated me, made me scared to tell anyone. He started the cycle of violence. I wish I had never met him. If I had never met him, the cycle of violence would never have happened. I wouldn't have been in the hospital with multiple complications. I wouldn't be in this rehab with foot drop, heart problems, and on dialysis.

In the hospital they found out my fistula was no good. When my blood is clean, they must either remove or revise the fistula, and if they remove it, I will need a new one. Three hospitalizations, two infections, and three surgeries in less than a year, and I didn't even want it. I'm heavily considering a hospice. I'm ruined. Dialysis is dictating my life. I'm so upset with the cycle of violence; I can't live like a normal person. My support system is limited.

I got my medical records after waiting for months; everything was as I predicted. I didn't have any drugs in my system besides the medications I have been prescribed. I did, however, find a piece of information that is alarming to me. I found out I had an early pregnancy or an ectopic pregnancy. I'm not going to go into all the details. But I found out. The documentation states the doctor notified the family and the psychiatrist said I couldn't make my wishes known. I was fully awake and alert on 4/14/22 when the test came back. My hormone levels were high and I had an ultrasound. My 'family' didn't notify me of this.

I really don't feel like I have a supportive family. No one knows my whole story. I mean that family member who I presume was the one notified was sitting straight across from me sometime that month, I think around that time to tell me they were moving my stuff from my apartment to my parents'. At least being pregnant I could have had hope and dreams and, who knows, maybe be alive to have the baby and have my own family.

I found out my ex-husband and his new wife had their baby on his birthday 12/14/22. I'm happy for him. I know he really wanted a baby. Now he has one. He will have someone to go to car events with. I know he's ecstatic.

I completed my final guest list for my birthday party—the second chance at life. I am a little disappointed. I thought I would have more people. No family are coming. I have received cancellations this week. But it's the quality that matters. My parents, I will see them on my actual birthday. Going to Ruth Chris with my angel and her husband for dinner on my birthday. And some can't come to the main event that Friday night, so I have a brunch that Sunday where they will be.

Text to Shawn on 12/19/22
Shawn and I texted the other day, but then he stopped replying. So I wrote him this:

I think your lack of response is a response, which makes me believe you don't want anything to do with me. You don't value me. You don't communicate or be honest or just talk with me anymore. I don't know what happened. I miss that. But your actions are showing you don't have the time or place for me in your life. So, I'm sorry, I can't wait. All I have is time, which makes me stay. But I don't want to waste more time on someone who doesn't want to be a part of my life. In 2023 big things are going to happen for me. I'm trying to focus on positive energy and company. I need to leave all of the people who hurt me back in 2022. I lost three best friends, my ex-husband, and you in the past 10 years. If communicating your feelings, if you have any for me, is hard for you, tell me. Don't leave me hanging like this. Otherwise I will have to move on from whatever we had. I'm sorry. I still love you unconditionally. I will always appreciate what you have done for me. But I need you to love me too. I have many battles to fight this year and one is going to have to be moving past you. I'm sorry. Maybe another time we'll meet. I wish you the best and happiness and a great holiday.

BETTER THINGS TO COME

2022 has been a struggle
So many battles I had to face, mostly alone
There are a few that helped me see the better
That there is more than a fight but to have fun

1995 I thought was the worst year of my life
Then 2020 I got a divorce and COVID symptoms for three months alone
I'm lucky I had good friends and family that were so nice
And the ones that pretended or didn't care are the ones that are gone

Smiles, laughter, getting those sweet messages and calls that were random
Just made my day a little brighter
Especially the ones that came down
Helped me be and see my fighter

2023 has good plans for me
I'm very optimistic. What you put in is what you get
It will let my past be free
It will let me sit back and be improved me

I had to go back to the hospital. I had five surgeries and eleven hospitalizations in the past year. My first love texted me hi, so I responded hi. I texted him a few days later and asked why he texted me. He said to wish me a happy new year. We texted for a bit and I sent him a funny video; he didn't respond for a couple of hours, so I asked him why. He said he was doing laundry. Three hours later, I asked if he saw it. He said he was busy. Later, he said he was working. I responded saying he said he was doing laundry. Then the silent treatment again. I texted him saying not to text or call if he didn't have a place for me in his life. The "I'm busy" I'm not going to tolerate.

CHAPTER 24

THE NEW YEAR

MY GOAL IS to do self-care, have peace, and only surround myself with people with matching energy. My friendships have changed. Some have gone missing and some became closer.

I'm happy that those who I'm not happy with I'm talking to and letting them know. I have peace, am drama free, and am sleeping better. Things are great for the new year. I can't wait to see what comes in the future.

ABOUT THE AUTHOR

MARAH REBECCA MALGAPO is a registered nurse with over 18 years of experience as a nurse. Worked on a medical-surgical, post-op, oncology, neuro floor, step down ICU, nursing home, homecare, hospice case management, school nurse, assisted living, administer vaccines, detox and dialysis. Marah has a passion for domestic violence, victims of being assaulted, homelessness for people and animals, and preventing animal abuse. When she is not working, she is listening to audiobooks, writing, poetry, and in the course of recovery. This is the first book she has written. Has a sequel in mind. Marah hopes her books can be a resource to other victims of assault.

RESOURCES

Abandonment Issues - Cognitive behavioral therapy (CBT)

Books for Children about Mental Health Issues - https://books2inspire.com

Crisis Text Line - Provides free, 24/7, confidential support via text message to people in crisis when they dial 741741

National Sexual Assault Hotline - A confidential and 24/7 support line 800-656-HOPE (4673)

RAINN - https://hotline.rainn.org/online for chatting about sexual assault

U.S. National Suicide Prevention Lifeline - 800-273-TALK (8255) any time, day or night, or chat online

CPSIA information can be obtained
at www.ICGtesting.com
Printed in the USA
LVHW020323060523
746236LV00010B/161